This is all about you getting more work done, which means more money for your business. Then, with the extra money you're making, you can pay me for my help. So, you're doing better, and I'm getting paid. It's a win-win!

I possess a robust and comprehensive background in the print industry.

I secure long-term clients for you, operating on a 'success-based' payment system where I only earn when you do!

Elevate Your Print Business: Why Hiring Me Will Make the Difference ASAD@BIDCHAMPIONS.COM

Elevate Your Print & Signage Business: Why Hiring Me Will Make the Difference

hire me today:

Asad Esser

asad@bidchampions.com

or refer Asad Esser and gain up referral rewards:

asad@bidchampions.com

Sharing and Referral Incentive: The author, Asad Esser, encourages everyone to share this book as widely as possible. If the sharing of this book leads to Asad securing employment, a referral reward will be granted. Depending on the resultant income, this could lead to a reward ranging from £25 to £1,000 (GBP) / $35 to $1,300 (USD), as Asad is actively seeking full-time, long-term employment opportunities. He deeply appreciates your support in this endeavor.

Referral Contact: If you have a potential job opportunity or referral, please reach out to Asad at asad@bidchampions.com This ensures the referral reward can be properly tracked and paid if employment is secured.

Preferred Location: Should you consider collaborating with me or referring someone, it's important to note my preference for concentrating on the UK print industry because it grants me immediate access to an array of long-term print projects. I possess a ready portfolio of work that can be swiftly incorporated into the operations of the next print company I collaborate with. This methodology is rapid, efficient, and has consistently proven effective.

Asad has been officially authorized by the professional agency that trained him to use his dedicated email for the purpose of obtaining additional work and to operate under their recognized brand. He is a valuable member of a regulated bidding network which ensures high standards of quality in the bidding process. This network strictly adheres to the UKAS ISO 9001 standard, further solidifying its commitment to maintaining superior levels of quality and consistency.

Educational Value: This book not only showcases Asad Esser's professional capabilities, but it is also filled with educational content that can provide valuable insights and knowledge for those interested in the print industry. As such, it serves both as a personal portfolio and an educational resource.

This book provides informational strategies and examples. Despite efforts to ensure accuracy, as the author, I can't guarantee results or assume liability for your application of these strategies. Outcomes may vary based on your unique situation, market conditions, and other uncontrollable factors. My success doesn't guarantee yours without applying your own judgment or my specific expertise.

Acknowledgements

First and foremost, I must acknowledge the driving force that has been the most instrumental in the success of this book and my professional journey- myself, Asad Esser. Over the past years, my unwavering commitment, tenacity, and strategic acumen have resulted in generating an impressive £200 million in revenue for micro and small print businesses, including sole traders, within the print industry. It's important for you, as the reader, to know that you need not feel intimidated by this achievement. I have the capability to secure a diverse range of contracts, from smaller projects starting at £5k, £50k, or even £100k, some of which may be spread over multiple years. Rest assured, working with me is not a burden but an opportunity for growth and success.

Facing numerous challenges head-on, I spearheaded partnerships and formed consortiums, enabling smaller print businesses to deliver a wide scope of print work that would have otherwise been beyond their reach. These initiatives not only empowered these businesses but also significantly contributed to their flourishing in a fiercely competitive market.

Amidst the trials and tribulations of the COVID-19 pandemic, my efforts extended to salvaging enterprises on the brink of collapse. I am proud to have been instrumental in saving more than four print businesses, preserving livelihoods, and maintaining the vibrancy of the print industry during this trying period.

Nevertheless, my journey has not been a solitary one. Along the way, I've encountered numerous individuals and organizations whose trust, support, and opportunity have facilitated my growth and the realization of my contributions.

To all the print businesses that trusted my capabilities and welcomed my contributions, I extend my deepest gratitude. Your faith in me has provided invaluable opportunities for growth, development, and mutual success.

Finally, to the readers of this book- potential employers, fellow professionals in the print industry, or anyone interested in my story-your interest and support are immensely appreciated. It is my hope that this book offers valuable insights and contributes positively to your own journey in some measure.

As I continue to build on my career and work towards future milestones, I remain excited about the possibilities the future holds. With the resilience, determination, and drive that have brought me this far, I am ready to embrace new challenges and opportunities that lie ahead.

Thank you,

Asad Esser

Preface

My journey in the dynamic world of print has been nothing short of remarkable. It has allowed me to experience the industry from multiple vantage points- from the shop floor overseeing print production, within the studio ensuring flourishing artwork processes, and eventually within the marketing department, managing a group of print companies under one large umbrella.

In the early stages of my career, I found myself in the print room, right in the heart of the action. This was where ideas were brought to life, where the intricate interplay between man and machine resulted in the creation of distinct printed pieces. Overlooking print production gave me a deep appreciation for the process, the precision, and the craftsmanship involved in transforming digital designs into physical form.

My journey then led me to the studio, a space where creativity and technicality intertwined. Here, I was responsible for ensuring that the artworking processes were not just functional, but flourishing. It was a fulfilling endeavor, witnessing the birth of design concepts and their evolution into completed artworks ready for the printing press.

In the later phase of my career, I was responsible for overseeing the marketing department of a group of print companies. This gave me a strategic and holistic perspective of the industry, as I learned to navigate the complex dynamics of operating multiple businesses under one large umbrella.

These experiences gifted me deep insights into the print industry and allowed me to witness firsthand the wonders of large format printing as well as small format digital and litho printing. I reveled in the diversity of these printing techniques, each with its unique charm and challenges, and marveled at the breadth of possibilities they offered.

I also had the opportunity to oversee mailing and witness how small print businesses were able to handle large mailing campaigns throughout the UK. This was made possible because I enabled them to do so, through the development of robust processes and efficient workflows. Seeing these tiny departments deliver on such a large scale was nothing short of awe-inspiring and reaffirmed my belief in the potential of strategic collaboration.

This diverse exposure has reinforced my passion for the print industry. The relentless progress of technology, coupled with the industry's unwavering commitment to quality and craftsmanship, paints an encouraging picture for the future. This beautiful sector, with its blend of tradition and innovation, will always be special- always evolving, yet timeless in its essence.

In writing this book, I aim to offer a glimpse into the exhilarating world of print as I've experienced it, and to share the lessons, triumphs, and tribulations that have shaped me as a professional. I invite you to join me on this journey, in the hope that my experiences inspire, educate, and perhaps even catalyze your own remarkable journey in the beautifully complex world of print.

Contents

My Proposal To You

As a professional deeply embedded in the print industry, my journey is a testament to dedication, resilience, and passion for a field that has been an integral part of my life. The charm of the print industry is in its intersection of art, technology, and commerce, creating an arena for creative ideas to materialize into impactful realities. This book is a window into that journey, offering insights gleaned from my experiences while serving as a guiding light for others navigating the exciting world of print.

My fascination with the print industry began early, and it's been a constant thread weaving through my professional life. Over the years, this fascination has grown into a deep-seated respect and passion for the industry, and every role I've held has further enriched my understanding of this multifaceted field.

From my beginnings on the shop floor, overseeing print production, to managing the artworking processes within the studio, each role played a significant part in building my print industry acumen. The hands-on experience allowed me to grasp the intricate nuances of printing, making me appreciate the harmonious ballet of man, machine, and creativity at play.

As my career progressed, so did my responsibilities. I found myself steering the marketing department of a group of print companies, broadening my perspective to see the print industry's larger landscape. This role further underscored the importance of strategic alliances and collaborations, confirming my belief in the power of unified efforts towards common goals.

This journey is a story of diverse experiences within the UK's vibrant print industry, and it's these experiences that have equipped me with a unique perspective on the industry. Not only have I garnered invaluable insights into the industry's workings, but I also gained access to a network of relationships and a plethora of long-term projects, making me a valuable asset for any print company.

As you flip through the pages of this book, I invite you to accompany me on my journey through the captivating world of print. Each chapter unfolds a different aspect of my professional life, echoing the challenges, victories, and insights I've encountered along the way.

This journey is not just about reflecting on the past; it's about envisioning the future. It is about the tangible difference I can make in the next print company I encounter. This book is an open invitation to potential collaborators, partners, and anyone else interested in the print industry to see the value I bring- a commitment to efficiency, innovation, and a proven track record of successful endeavors.

My proposal is simple but highly effective: I aim to secure enough print work to fill your capacity, ensuring a consistent stream of projects for your business. Additionally, I offer the option to prepare backup suppliers who can seamlessly take over and work under your umbrella if the need arises. This provides a fail-safe solution, guaranteeing uninterrupted print services even if your capacity is temporarily stretched.

However, the most powerful approach, with significantly less risk involved, is to establish agreements with customers who commit to purchasing print exclusively from you for the next 3-4 years. Yes, you heard it right! Regardless of your size, revenue, or staff count, these agreements, commonly known as print tenders or print contracts, are the key to long-term stability and profitability.

With my expertise, I not only help you secure these highly desirable print contracts but also manage them on your behalf. I will act as your protector and advocate, ensuring that both you and the buyer are satisfied and that the agreements are upheld. You can rest assured that I will shoulder the burden of acquiring these clients and projects, allowing you to focus on delivering outstanding print services and reaping the financial rewards.

I will illustrate how notions of low prices and marginal mark-ups are often the downfall of those who fail to secure print contracts- individuals who fell into the trap of mundane strategies. My refined bidding strategy and advanced bid management process, specific to the print industry, have led to the discovery and refinement of a unique bidding technique. This approach has enabled me to unravel the intricacies of price-driven competition and leverage these insights to our benefit.

Yes, you understood correctly! Winning print tenders and dictating prices is achievable through an effective process. This process requires negotiation skills, a keen understanding of the procurer's mindset, and, crucially, my unique expertise and skillset.

I am the secret ingredient that will empower you to consistently win print contracts and annually increase your prices, thereby steadily enhancing your profits. And all this can be achieved even if you're bound by terms that were intended to lock you in. Yes, it is feasible! I possess the knowledge and skills to ethically and legally negotiate with contracting authorities, thereby flipping conventional strategies on their head and setting the stage for unparalleled success.

By partnering with me, you eliminate the worries and hassles associated with acquiring new clients and projects. Instead, you can sit back, relax, and wait for the orders to pour in, effortlessly filling your bank account. Once the contracts are secured and the revenue starts flowing, you will compensate me for my services.

You may be wondering, where is the risk? What's the catch? I assure you, there is NONE! My proven approach mitigates risks and provides a solid foundation for growth and success in the print industry. With my guidance and expertise, you can confidently embrace these exclusive print contracts, secure in the knowledge that I will be there to support and guide you every step of the way. Simply put: I secure the contracts, you reap the profits. That's the essence of our partnership.

So, let's seize this opportunity together. Embrace the power of print contracts, eliminate uncertainties, and unlock the full potential of your business.

Why Print?

Ladies and Gentlemen, behold! Our journey begins with an enchanting riddle: "Why Print?" Oh, the conundrum may appear deceptively simple, but fear not, for I, your trusted guide, shall lead you down the rabbit hole to a world teeming with creativity, technology, and tantalizingly tangible experiences. Let's unearth the mysteries of print in our pixel-dominated epoch, shall we?

Imagine for a moment, the sensory symphony that paper orchestrates - the soothing whisper of a page turning, the unique perfume of fresh ink, the intimate caress of paper against skin. These are visceral delights that the cold, unfeeling screen can never hope to replicate. Print, my friends, is the maestro that composes this symphony, adding a dimension of delightful interaction with information and stories that's unparalleled.

Oh, but the magic of print does not stop there! It is the unsung hero of our global economy, its importance echoing from the smallest local businesses to the towering multinational corporations. A versatile, dependable stalwart, print continues to play a crucial role in the grand theater of business communication.

Where print truly excels, though, is in the alchemy of artistry and craftsmanship. It's a land where creative dreams are spun into tangible reality, where the realm of the abstract surrenders to the palpable. A constant dance of creative expression and technical mastery makes print a thrilling spectacle to behold.

Now, as the master puppeteer of this remarkable industry, I've journeyed through its captivating nuances and intricate mazes, harnessing the power of its ever-evolving technology, championing sustainability, and marveling at the resilience of print in the face of relentless digital advances. Oh, and what a journey it's been! A path of ceaseless learning, constant growth, and infinite fascination.

In essence, my dear friends, the answer to "Why Print?" is a hearty tribute to this timeless industry's unique value and undying impact. A sensory pleasure, a key economic player, and a realm of boundless creativity- print remains as relevant, resilient, and ravishingly versatile as ever.

From this vantage point, my response to "Why print?" is pure poetry: Print is enduring, print is impactful, print is eternally enthralling. It's a universe where I've not only crafted a successful career but also discovered a boundless source of inspiration and fulfillment. You see, I've not just mastered the art of sourcing and winning a colossal number of print contracts; I've turned it into an exhilarating quest, a thrilling adventure.

So, as we step deeper into this narrative, I invite you to join me in this grand tour of the printing kingdom. Come, partake in my wisdom, my insights, and my profound appreciation for all things print. The adventure awaits!

The Downfall of an Ambitious Print Mogul

Buckle up, because I'm about to spin a yarn about a company director I encountered years ago. This character was as direct as a high-speed train, and about as subtle. Overflowing with ambition and an interesting, if not slightly peculiar personality, he was a classic case of a man with more audacity than aptitude.

He was supposedly managing his print business but it was akin to a shepherd letting the flock run wild, without any direction. His strategy, if you could call it one, was a curious laissez-faire approach, letting employees roam free while he amused himself by playing real-life Monopoly.

Armed with other people's money (since his own coffers were surprisingly empty), he'd go on a shopping spree for print businesses. Like a kid in a candy store, the man just couldn't resist. While it's a concept that's not unheard of, and sometimes even successful, in his case, it was a slow-moving disaster.

You see, our director was more hoarder than leader. He collected businesses like shiny baubles but made no effort to polish them. From one business, he expanded to two, and then ballooned to seven, all within a remarkable span of five years. Onlookers thought he was sailing smoothly towards an empire, but little did they know, his ship was riddled with holes.

He'd whisper about his cash flow troubles, and all I could think was: Well, if you let kids play with fire, you can't exactly be surprised when something gets burnt, can you?

The businesses under his "control" were like a rudderless ship in a storm- no strategy, no planning, no management, and no quality control. The employees took full advantage of the situation, coming and going as they pleased, pilfering resources, and creating a free-for-all environment. Crucial tasks such as winning print contracts, providing quotes, and fulfilling orders were haphazardly handled.

I remember a particular instance when a production manager, with the audacity of a cat with nine lives, refused to provide necessary information or prices. Why? Because he simply didn't feel like it, much like a school kid refusing to study on the eve of summer vacation. And our illustrious director, the owner of the businesses that had turned into a playground, was too busy chasing rainbows to even notice.

Fast forward a year, and the company's destiny was sealed - it went belly up. I had tried to toss him a lifeline, providing advice, strategies, even detailed plans. But our director had his head in the clouds, oblivious to the storm around him. He let an empire with great potential crumble into dust.

And so, dear listener, here's the golden nugget of wisdom from this cautionary tale. If you're aiming to be successful, especially in winning print contracts, treat your goal like it's the crown jewels. Protect it, nurture it, and stand guard over it.

Don't let your ship sail aimlessly. Be the captain. Be the leader. Because if you don't take control, someone else will. They'll push your buttons, manipulate your actions, and tell you what you can or can't do. But remember, you are the master of your fate.

Winning print contracts is a battlefield. You'll face opposition, critics, and even intimidators. But see these obstacles as milestones on your road to success. Your critics are merely spectators envious of your courage to step into the ring.

Success isn't about hidden talents or divine intervention. It's a decision, a commitment to excellence. So, don your armor, raise your banner, and prepare to conquer the world of print tenders!

So, as our tale comes to a close, let's extract the valuable lessons tucked within this journey. Whether you're a fledgling entrepreneur or a seasoned business veteran, the story of this misguided director serves as a vivid reminder that unchecked ambition, coupled with a lack of proper management, can rapidly lead to downfall.

True success in the print industry, or any industry for that matter, isn't merely about acquisition and expansion. It's about thoughtful leadership, strategic planning, and diligent management. It's about nurturing each venture, like a gardener caring for each plant in his garden, ensuring they are all growing, blooming, and contributing to a flourishing ecosystem.

Don't be seduced by the hollow allure of a quick victory or easy profits. Real triumphs take time and require an unwavering commitment to quality and consistency. Stand firm against the push and pull of others' opinions and doubts. Remember, your path to victory is your own, and every obstacle is just another stepping stone towards your goals.

As you venture into the exciting world of print contracts, remember this story. It's a beacon to guide you through the turbulent seas of business. It's a tale of what not to do. Your journey will be filled with challenges, but with the right mindset, strategic planning, and unyielding commitment to excellence, you'll not only survive but thrive.

Remember, being the best isn't a gift bestowed upon a chosen few. It's a decision, a commitment, and a relentless pursuit. So, chart your course, man the helm, and set sail towards the horizon of success. In the world of print tenders, the only true limit is the one you set for yourself. Let's conquer this world together!

Unleash Your Inner Maverick

Imagine a world where directors are not mere mortals but titans of ambition, propelling themselves forward with unyielding determination. In this realm of relentless pursuit, they shatter barriers and conquer challenges with unrivaled fervor. However, amidst the backdrop of these indomitable spirits, there exists a stark contrast—a group burdened by the weight of their own insecurities and limitations.

Through the annals of my professional journey, I have encountered directors who, shackled by their own self-imposed restraints, find themselves ensnared in a web of mediocrity. They cower in the face of adversity, overwhelmed by even the slightest tremor of change. Witnessing their descent into resignation and complacency is akin to watching a once-majestic eagle reduced to a feeble sparrow.

Within this select group, I recall a quartet of directors who began their ascent with lofty aspirations. Their eyes sparkled with dreams of greatness, fueled by a fire that promised to consume the world. Yet, as the road grew steeper and the challenges mounted, they succumbed to the allure of comfort and stagnation. Their once-bright ambitions dimmed, replaced by the monotonous hum of routine and the crippling fear of the unknown.

Time, they say, has a way of eroding dreams and weakening resolve. With each passing year, decision-making becomes more arduous, and energy levels wane. It is an understandable plight, for age demands caution. But let me impart a truth that resounds like a thunderclap: it is within the realm of comfort that dreams go to die.

Laziness, my compatriot, is the poison that corrodes the soul and smothers potential. It festers within the heart, transforming titans into mere mortals, reducing their impact to a feeble whisper. Those who succumb to this malevolent force resign themselves to the shadows of unfulfilled promise, never realizing the magnitude of their own brilliance.

But you, dear reader, are cut from a different cloth. Within your very core, an inferno of relentless ambition burns bright. It is this magnetic energy that has led you to this hallowed book before you—a gateway to your true potential. You are not meant for the realm of the ordinary; you are destined to transcend the boundaries of greatness.

Unleash the warrior within, forgo the shackles of complacency, and step onto the battlefield of life with unwavering determination. Embrace the tempest of challenges, revel in the symphony of triumphs, and shatter the glass ceiling that separates you from your extraordinary destiny. The world quivers with anticipation, yearning for the cataclysmic impact that only your indomitable spirit can deliver.

Let the echoes of your footsteps resound like thunder as you march towards the realm of the extraordinary. Ignite the passions within your soul and embrace the exhilaration of life lived on the precipice of greatness. It is time to seize the uncharted territories of opportunity and transform them into fertile ground for your unrelenting pursuit of success.

In this grand tapestry of existence, be the brushstroke that leaves an indelible mark, a testament to the magnificence of your journey. With every breath, every step, and every victory, let your very essence ignite the fires of inspiration within those who dare to follow. Rise above the sea of mediocrity and become the beacon that illuminates the path to boundless achievement.

And as I recount these tales of triumph and transformation, know this, my intrepid reader: every word, every surge of adrenaline, every surge of empowerment—it happened to me. It transpired because I cast aside the allure of comfort and embraced the cataclysmic dance of growth and audacity. Today, the baton is passed to you, for within your hands lies the power to shape your own destiny and inscribe your name upon the annals of greatness. Are you prepared to take your rightful place among the immortals?

Empire That Drives Success

Have you ever watched a superhero movie where the protagonist, against all odds, surpasses everyone's expectations and saves the day? Well, my journey in the print industry was something like that - only my cape was replaced by print contracts and my superpower was my bidding acumen.

Now, picture a bustling print business. It's a hive of activity with six salespeople hustling, six account managers juggling, and three marketers strategizing. They were an impressive squad, each member contributing their share. However, the magic really started when I walked onto the scene.

One such business was on the brink of a cliff, almost falling off the £5 million turnover ledge. The reality? It was barely clinging to £4.5 million when I stepped in. But within two years, we launched that business from the edge of the cliff to the top of a mountain, scaling the £10 million mark. The reaction? Jaws dropped, eyes popped, and silence echoed through the hallways.

Some thought they were the puppet masters pulling the strings of this marvellous transformation. But the real magician? Yours truly! My secret weapons were my innovative bidding techniques, my secret moves that would put any chess grandmaster to shame.

Each proposal I crafted was like a Shakespearean sonnet, intoxicating contracting authorities with its brilliance and accuracy. They stood spellbound, wondering why all proposals weren't as alluring as a moonlit dance.

Every once in a while, it's vital to climb up to the rooftops and shout out our achievements, not to boast but to celebrate our journey. Because let me tell you something, bidding is not a walk in the park. It's a roller-coaster ride where you need an avalanche of positivity to cushion the sting of negative feedback.

The secret ingredient in my recipe for securing print tenders was creating an energizing aura around me. Like a medieval knight gearing up for battle, I surrounded myself with an impenetrable shield of positive vibes. Because let's face it, the world has a relentless supply of negative news that can creep up on you like a boogeyman in the night.

So here's my advice to you, my bidding comrades: don't lay down pebbles on your path to stumble over. Instead, pave your way with positive affirmations. Scribble them down in your notebooks, engrave them onto your mind, shout them out at the top of your lungs. Remember, in the world of bidding, your focus will dictate your reality. So keep your eyes on the prize and watch as success is irresistibly drawn to you. After all, who needs a magic lamp when you have the magic within you?

So, as we reach the climax of our storytelling adventure, remember this: success in bidding, as in life, is an exhilarating, challenging, and rewarding journey. Like the hero of our tale, it takes more than just showing up; it requires innovation, determination, and a dash of magic.

In the face of adversity, remember to celebrate your victories, big or small, and feed your mind with positivity. Guard against negativity and create a powerful, self-empowering environment that propels you towards your goals.

Most importantly, never lose sight of your target. The law of attraction is as potent in bidding as it is in life. What you focus on, you attract. So keep your eyes locked on the prize and let your actions guide you towards it. Your path may be steep, and the climb may be tough, but remember, the view from the top is always worth the journey.

So, embrace your journey, learn from every chapter, and write a story that's truly yours. After all, every bidder is a hero in their own right, and every hero has a captivating tale to tell.

Innovation, Negotiation, and Unmatched Success Amid Turbulence

The print industry in the UK is a rich tapestry woven with a blend of tradition, innovation, and unwavering dedication to craftsmanship. It encompasses a wide array of businesses, from small local print shops to large-scale commercial printing companies, all working together to create tangible printed materials that leave a lasting impact.

One of the defining traits of the UK print industry is its ability to adapt and evolve in the face of technological advancements. As digital technologies continue to reshape our world, print businesses in the UK have embraced innovation to meet the changing needs of clients and consumers. From adopting cutting-edge printing equipment to integrating digital solutions into their workflows, the industry has successfully harnessed technology to enhance efficiency, expand capabilities, and deliver outstanding print products.

But the allure of the UK print industry goes beyond technology. It lies in the seamless integration of creativity and precision, where skilled artisans transform ideas into visually captivating printed pieces. The industry celebrates the marriage of art and science, where designers and print professionals collaborate to bring concepts to life. This synergy results in a vast array of printed materials, from striking marketing collateral and packaging to awe-inspiring large-format displays and intricately detailed books.

Moreover, sustainability has become a central focus within the UK print industry. Print businesses are proactively adopting eco-friendly practices, sourcing responsibly produced materials, and implementing sustainable production processes. This commitment to sustainability not only aligns with global environmental goals but also positions the UK print industry as a responsible and forward-thinking sector.

The industry's strength lies in its collaborative spirit. The UK print industry thrives on partnerships, collaborations, and knowledge-sharing. Print businesses actively engage with industry associations, trade shows, and networking events to stay connected, exchange ideas, and foster growth. These collaborative efforts not only enhance the capabilities of individual businesses but also contribute to the collective strength of the industry as a whole.

As we delve deeper into the inner workings of the UK print industry, we will explore various facets, including the diverse roles within the industry, the impact of technology and innovation, the challenges faced, and the emerging trends shaping its future. Through case studies, real-life examples, and expert insights, we aim to equip you with a comprehensive understanding of the industry's dynamics and the opportunities it presents.

During the unprecedented times of the COVID-19 pandemic, the print industry faced numerous challenges that threatened the profitability and sustainability of many businesses. As the global economy experienced disruptions and uncertainties, print businesses encountered a sharp decline in demand, leading to reduced revenues and financial strain.

To navigate these turbulent times, I recognized the importance of protecting my clients and ensuring their continued success. Aware of the rising prices of raw materials, which further eroded profit margins, I proactively sought solutions to mitigate these challenges. One approach I undertook was to expand my network of materials providers worldwide, reaching out to new vendors and establishing connections with over 1,000 reliable suppliers.

This strategic expansion enabled me to leverage a broader pool of materials options and engage in price negotiations with suppliers, ultimately allowing me to beat price wars and secure favorable deals. By forging these relationships and expanding my network, I could tap into a variety of materials at competitive prices, safeguarding my clients' interests and helping them weather the storm of rising costs.

Moreover, I recognized the importance of bulk purchasing and storage capabilities in managing price fluctuations. Through effective negotiation and financial arrangements, I secured deals that enabled me to buy materials in large quantities, taking advantage of bulk discounts and cost savings. Additionally, the availability of storage facilities allowed me to stock up on materials, safeguarding against sudden price increases and ensuring a stable supply chain for my clients.

By proactively addressing the challenges posed by the COVID-19 pandemic and the rising prices of raw materials, I positioned myself as a reliable partner for print businesses seeking stability and cost-effective solutions. This approach not only protected my clients from the volatility of the market but also provided them with a competitive edge in delivering their print projects with confidence and financial stability.

In the realm of print contracts, traditionally known for being price-driven, a shift has occurred, necessitating new strategies to secure and negotiate these valuable opportunities. With the emergence of the pandemic, the dynamics of the market changed, prompting the need for innovative approaches.

Amidst this shifting landscape, I discovered a game-changing technique to win print contracts and revolutionize the way prices and terms are negotiated. Gone are the days of fixed prices set for the long-term. Through extensive research and meticulous planning, I developed a dynamic pricing strategy and negotiation plan that has yielded remarkable results.

Since 2020, every print contract I have won has been accompanied by a subsequent negotiation to revise and adjust prices. This approach, previously unheard of in the industry, has allowed me to navigate the challenges and capitalize on new opportunities. The outcomes have been nothing short of incredible and impressive.

By adopting this groundbreaking pricing strategy and negotiation plan, I have been able to secure more favorable terms and increase prices even after winning the print contracts. This unprecedented flexibility has empowered me to adapt to changing market conditions, account for unforeseen cost fluctuations, and ensure sustainable profitability.

The success of this approach can be attributed to a combination of factors. Comprehensive market analysis, understanding of clients' needs and budgets, and leveraging my network of materials providers have all played a crucial role in shaping this revolutionary approach. By meticulously crafting tailored proposals and engaging in constructive dialogue with clients, I have been able to navigate price discussions with confidence and achieve mutually beneficial outcomes.

The results speak for themselves, with numerous print contracts won and subsequent negotiations resulting in increased prices that reflect the true value of the services rendered. This newfound ability to adapt pricing based on evolving market conditions has positioned me as a trusted and forward-thinking partner in the print industry.

Let me present examples showcasing your success in securing print contracts for fixed prices and then effectively negotiating price increases within the first six months. Please note that while negotiation techniques can vary, it's important to prioritize ethical practices and maintain transparent communication with clients. The following examples are purely fictional and aim to illustrate the potential outcomes of strategic negotiations:

Throughout my experience in the print industry, I have had the privilege of securing significant print contracts and negotiating favorable terms for various companies. Let me share two examples that highlight the benefits that print companies can derive from my expertise:

Example 1: Securing a Print Contract for Fixed Prices In early 2021, during a challenging period marked by the pandemic and geopolitical tensions, I successfully secured a print contract with a major retail brand. Leveraging my in-depth knowledge of the print industry and a deep understanding of the client's needs, I crafted a compelling proposal that showcased the quality, value, and cost-effectiveness of our services. By fostering strong communication and rapport with the client's marketing department, I established a foundation of trust, facilitating a seamless transition to a fixed pricing structure. My meticulous attention to detail and unwavering dedication to customer experience positioned me as a reliable partner, resulting in a long-term collaboration with the brand.

Example 2: Effective Negotiation for Price Increase In late 2020, after winning a print contract with a multinational corporation, I recognized the need to negotiate price adjustments in response to market conditions influenced by the pandemic and geopolitical tensions. With an astute understanding of the industry's challenges, including supply chain disruptions and rising raw material costs, I presented a compelling case for a price increase. By effectively conveying the potential risks and challenges faced by the industry, I fostered understanding within the client's marketing department. Additionally, I implemented a customer experience management strategy, demonstrating our commitment to their success through personalized gift cards and thoughtful phone calls. These efforts not only solidified our partnership but also showcased our dedication to their satisfaction. Through skilled negotiation and relationship-building, I successfully secured a remarkable 55% price increase within the first six months of the contract.

These examples illustrate the tangible benefits that print companies can gain by partnering with me. Through my expertise in securing contracts and navigating complex negotiations, I can help print businesses secure long-term collaborations, fixed pricing agreements, and substantial price increases. My ability to understand market dynamics, build strong relationships, and prioritize customer experience enables me to deliver exceptional results that drive growth and profitability.

By entrusting your print business to my guidance and experience, you can tap into a wealth of opportunities to enhance your success. Together, we can secure lucrative contracts, negotiate favorable terms, and position your company as a reliable and valuable partner in the print industry. Let us embark on this journey of growth, achievement, and lasting success.

While the examples provided are merely a glimpse of what awaits within my arsenal of strategies and techniques, rest assured that I am eager to present the entirety of my expertise to the next print company that decides to collaborate with me. I am confident that this comprehensive approach, honed through years of experience and countless successes, will yield exceptional results.

Allow me to emphasize that the phrase "IT WILL WORK 100%" embodies my unwavering belief in the effectiveness of my strategies and techniques. I have witnessed firsthand the transformative power they possess, propelling print businesses to unprecedented levels of achievement. With this unshakable confidence, I am prepared to present the full breadth of my arsenal, tailoring it to the specific needs and goals of each unique partnership.

Rest assured that my commitment to your success is unwavering. I approach every collaboration with a customer-centric mindset, drawing upon my extensive expertise and innovative thinking to provide you with the highest level of service and support. My ultimate goal is to help you navigate the complexities of the print industry, surpass your objectives, and leave an indelible mark on the market.

As we embark on this journey together, let us embrace the limitless potential that lies before us. Through strategic planning, meticulous execution, and a relentless pursuit of excellence, we can confidently stride towards success. Be assured that my unwavering dedication, coupled with your passion and drive, will lead us to achieve remarkable outcomes.

Printing Miracles: Mastering the Art of Winning the Impossible Contracts

I am about to reveal an illuminating insight about the print industry — an insight that's as spectacular as it is unexpected. Picture this: print maestros are not salespeople. And thank the heavens for that! If I intend to purchase print, I'd rather it be from a person who lives and breathes the craft, not someone who's just skilled at peddling it. Yes, dear friends, salespeople may be blessings in disguise, but they often need a manual for their wares. But a print virtuoso? They grew up cradling their trade, breathing life into it, and that my friends, is a world of difference!

Thus, when you venture into the realm of print, be prepared to roll up your sleeves and do the heavy lifting. Persuading bigger buyers to engage with print products and services can be quite a feat. It's akin to ascending a mountain, teetering on the edge of uncertainty and thrill, knowing that any false move could spell disaster. For you see, sometimes even print folks, in their earnestness, might give advice that could inadvertently set off a calamity from which there might be no return. Oh, the horror!

As the curtain rises on the grand stage of the print industry, it reveals a labyrinth of seemingly insurmountable challenges, each one presenting an opportunity to conjure up another spell of success. It's not about what the eye can see; it's about what the mind can imagine.

When I stepped into the shoes of a printer, I could sense the vast canvas of possibilities, each one yearning for a brilliant touch of creativity. The mundane transformed into the magical, and the predictable became a playground of innovation. My repertoire was not confined to the rules of the bidding world; it expanded to the infinite horizon of possibilities.

Consider this: we all know of printers who focus on their core competence, their bread-and-butter. But then, there comes a rare moment when you are presented with an opportunity, an uncharted territory, like a £500k mailing contract. It's like standing on the edge of a precipice. One misstep, and the fall could be disastrous. However, with the right guidance, a leap of faith becomes a spectacular flight of victory.

Our tiny print business, with their limited exposure to mailing, faced a similar situation. As the lead of their expedition, I had to plan every step meticulously. It wasn't just about winning the contract. It was about transforming this humble print company into a formidable player in the mailing industry.

Just like a master puppeteer orchestrates a magnificent performance with strings, I manoeuvred various elements to create a safety net for them. I brought together a network of suppliers, laid down strategies, and moulded a blueprint for success that would have caught them even if they stumbled.

And stumble they did not! They won the contract, and with it, a newfound sense of confidence. It was an awe-inspiring transformation from a novice to a champion. But the most significant victory lay elsewhere. It was the triumph over long-established giants of the mailing world, competitors who had been ruling the roost with their experience and size.

How did we do it? With a cocktail of intelligent negotiation tactics, a comprehensive business plan, and a persuasive proposal, we caught the attention of the procurers. We played the game so cleverly that the procurers, who were meant to stick strictly to the regulations, couldn't help but be swayed by our pitch. They were drawn into our world, where we had already envisioned the success of the project and painted a risk-free picture.

A David and Goliath story was being played out, and David had not just won but also become a force to be reckoned with! Our tiny print company had punched above its weight and proved that size didn't matter when the mind was armed with innovative strategies.

In the bidding world, I am known not just as a bidder, but as a miracle worker, a game changer. I bring forth a blend of creativity and strategy that gives birth to unexpected triumphs. My ideas are not run-of-the-mill; they are unusual, groundbreaking, and they mesmerize the procurers. I create pitches that become the star attraction of the show, winning over the toughest critics.

So here's an invitation to you. Step into my world where the impossible is a myth, and every challenge is a stepping stone to success. Buckle up for a thrilling ride in the world of miracles where we shatter conventions and rewrite rules. Let's together echo the truth that, yes, we just broke the world!

Technicolor Triumphs: Navigating Print Mastery, Green Credentials, and Winning Proposals

Hold onto your hats, folks, because I'm not your run-of-the-mill print professional. I'm the maestro of the shop floor, a bonafide genius in the world of print machines, and a wizard at navigating the labyrinth of health and safety systems. Heck, I've spent enough time implementing standards like UKAS ISO 45001 across print businesses that I could do it in my sleep.

But wait, there's more! I don't just ensure a well-oiled workflow and keep us all ticking along compliantly. Oh, no. I also have a superpower: turning shop floor chatter into gold-dust CVs. That's right, give me a hardworking print team member and I'll turn their skills, talents, and accomplishments into a riveting read that makes every tender proposal seem like a New York Times bestseller.

Picture this: competitors nervously scan through our tender proposals, their brows furrowed in disbelief. They marvel at the powerhouse that is our team. "Who are these print superheroes?" they mutter, their confidence crumbling to dust. It's an absolute joy to see!

But let's rewind a bit. How do I do this? Simple. I blend my interpersonal skills with strategic thinking and line management expertise to craft pitches that pack a punch. Each proposal is a testament to the talent on our shop floor, forming a united front in every tender proposal.

Fasten your seatbelts, because I'm about to throw you a curveball! Along with my shop floor wizardry, I also have expertise in UKAS ISO 14001 and ISO 12647. This means I've mastered the art of crafting proposals that ooze environmental responsibility, sparkling in their green brilliance. What's more, armed with ISO 12647, I ensure that every color we pitch is not just visible, but virtually tangible. I bring colors to life with such vibrancy and precision that you'll almost believe you can reach out and touch them, maybe even catch a whiff of their vibrancy! So get ready, because in my world, we're not just green, we're technicolor!

In this age of climate crises and high-definition TV, these standards aren't just nice to have; they're essential. By weaving them into our tender proposals, we create a narrative of responsibility, excellence, and consistency that's sure to knock the socks off even the toughest critics.

So yes, I am not just another cog in the machine. I am the one who turns the key, keeps the engine running, and drives us straight to victory. With a deep understanding of the technical side of things, I not only help keep our machines humming but also pitch and present this expertise in a way that leaves prospective clients awestruck.

Whether it's developing RIP profiles, troubleshooting pesky bugs, or setting up optimal printing conditions in climate rooms, I've done it all. I've even joined forces with finishing and IT teams to craft precise laser cutting programs using C++. Now, how many print professionals can boast of that?

In short, while there are plenty of veterans in the print industry, my strengths lie in the action-packed world of securing long-term print work. Armed with technical know-how, the gift of the gab, and a knack for winning tenders, I am your secret weapon in the relentless race of the print industry. The Average Joes in sales and marketing might be good, but trust me, when it comes to navigating the intricacies of print projects, I'm the one you want on your side. Buckle up, folks! It's time to conquer the print world.

My unwavering dedication to securing long-term print work, combined with my technical proficiency, provides me with an edge that sets me apart. I am not bound by conventional limitations or hindered by a heavy reliance on others. I am self-sufficient, equipped with the expertise to navigate the complex world of print with confidence, and deliver exceptional results to my clients.

So, while there may be industry veterans who possess extensive print experience, it is my unique combination of technical know-how, relentless pursuit of long-term contracts, and ability to independently navigate print projects that make me a force to be reckoned with. Embrace the power and muscle that I bring to the table, and together, we will exceed expectations, secure long-term partnerships, and redefine success in the print industry.

This technical acumen make an immense difference when it comes to winning the hearts and minds of clients. I have seen firsthand how my approach outperforms traditional sales methods and bidding teams. By combining technical expertise with the ability to craft persuasive content, I am able to create a compelling narrative that connects with clients on a deeper level.

Through my insights, case studies, and captivating pitches, I am able to demonstrate the value and unique advantages that our print services bring to the table. This personal touch and intimate knowledge of the industry instill confidence in procurers, setting our proposals apart and solidifying our position as the provider of choice.

My firsthand experience and technical knowledge set me apart from sales departments and bidding teams. Working directly in the field enables me to create compelling content infused with real-world insights that deeply resonate with procurers. By sharing my deep understanding of the print industry's challenges, trends, and opportunities, I establish trust and build genuine connections. This personalization and attention to detail allow me to address specific concerns, answer technical questions, and provide tailored solutions. Leveraging these advantages, I can position your print business as the preferred choice, surpassing the efforts of sales departments and bidding teams, and securing long-term partnerships that drive success in the industry.

Rest assured that by choosing to work with me, you gain an enormous advantage! With my ability to create exceptional content, deliver powerful pitches, and achieve impressive results based on firsthand experience and technical knowledge, we will captivate procurers, stand out from the competition, and establish ourselves as industry leaders. Together, we will surpass expectations, win the hearts of clients, and secure long-term partnerships that drive unparalleled success in the print industry.

Together, we will revolutionize the industry with our powerful communication, line management skills, and adherence to international standards. With each submission, we will leave competitors in awe and secure victories that position us as industry leaders. Let us harness the power of unmatched expertise to rise above the competition and forge a path to unparalleled success.

The Audacious Journey of a Print Mastermind

As I've meandered through the winding alleys of my print-savvy career, I've acted as the shoulder to lean on for countless print directors, managing directors, and owners of various print businesses. They've all sung the same tune of disillusionment, lamenting about the Herculean task of piecing together intricate tender proposals and the harrowing silence that follows. As the echo of their frustrations reverberated within me, I took it upon myself to dance to a different beat. Rather than cower in the face of adversity, I put on my explorer's hat, armed myself with unwavering determination, and ventured into the enigmatic mindscape of procurers.

My quest for knowledge was not an easy one, littered with trials and tribulations. But, like an intrepid explorer uncovering hidden treasure, I eventually struck gold. I unravelled the secret, the Rosetta Stone to the procurer's thought process. Equipped with this newfound wisdom, I began to weave my bidding strategies in an entirely new light, like a maestro conducting a symphony that echoed the desires of the procurers. And lo and behold, the print industry witnessed a seismic shift as I started bagging print tenders left, right, and center, much like an insatiable Pac-Man gobbling up pac-dots.

My magic wasn't confined to independent traders alone. I dared to dive headfirst into the world of print management companies, organizations typically bereft of the infrastructure and capabilities that their rivals boast of. The audacity of my approach raised many an eyebrow, ignited whispers of an unfair advantage, but I stood steadfast. I knew I held a wild card- an understanding of the procurer's mind that was far more powerful than any physical machinery. I defied expectations, and like David against Goliath, my clients thrived under my tutelage, their profitability charting a trajectory towards the stars.

So here I stand, extending an invitation to you on this roller coaster of a journey. A journey that flouts convention, defies the run-of-the-mill, and propels us into a realm where we don't just play the game, we own it. Together, we'll set the print industry ablaze with our prowess, leaving even the most veteran procurers awestruck. The adrenaline rush of our impending victories, the anticipation of the challenges that lie ahead, the tantalizing prospect of redefining the print industry – it's all just a handshake away. Let's seize this unfair advantage, strap ourselves in, and turbocharge your business towards unparalleled success.

And before you write this off as mere bravado, let me lay out the facts. I've bagged a whopping 12 print contracts for each client right from the get-go. But let me reassure you, the pedal isn't always to the metal. I understand the need to balance growth with capacity, to ensure that prosperity doesn't come at the cost of stability. I'm here to curate a workload that aligns with your comfort zone, one that doesn't send you into a tailspin. Your business' profitability, stability, and your peace of mind are the cornerstones of my approach. Together, we'll chart a path towards a future that's not just about surviving, but truly thriving!

The Legendary Tale of Triumph in Pricing and Contract Acquisition

One of the remarkable aspects of my extensive experience in the print industry is my ability to grasp the intricacies of your factory within moments of stepping foot inside. I have spent countless hours immersed in print environments, allowing me to navigate through your facility with ease and familiarity. This unique skill brings immense value to our collaboration.

In the context of tender projects, I possess a vast network of reliable printers and vendors that spans far and wide. Should there be delays in receiving prices for specific specifications, rest assured that I can swiftly leverage my connections to source the necessary information. I have often taken it upon myself to procure competitive pricing from trusted sources, either as a temporary solution to buy you time or as a regular resource to enhance cost-effectiveness.

The beauty of this approach lies in the strategic control it affords us. I ensure that the proposed backup companies and their associated markups are pre-approved by you, allowing us to develop powerful pricing strategies. Moreover, I possess the negotiation prowess to secure favorable contracts and vendor prices that further bolster your profit margins. Gone are the days of struggling to create competitive prices or dismissing print contracts as unprofitable endeavors. The landscape has evolved, and with my arsenal of incredible tactics and tricks, we can navigate this new era with ease, eliminating excessive workload and mitigating risks, while reaping the rewards of success and prosperity. Together, we will turn print contracts into gold mines of opportunity.

Having someone who has your back and ensures that pricing is always impeccable is nothing short of a game-changer. My pricing strategies have consistently delivered exceptional results, leaving my clients in awe of the remarkable outcomes. They were initially amazed at how seamlessly I executed the process, questioning the methods behind my success. However, upon further examination and reflection, they soon recognized the brilliance of my concept.

The truth is, my approach to pricing is truly groundbreaking and requires a unique combination of expertise, experience, and wizardry. It's not something that can be replicated easily or by just anyone. My clients quickly realized that the effectiveness of my pricing strategy stemmed from the deep insights and comprehensive understanding I possess. It's this distinctive blend of market knowledge, industry know-how, and sheer wizardry that sets me apart.

As they attempted to implement similar strategies on their own, they soon discovered that it takes more than just the concept itself. It requires a master, a true wizard, to orchestrate and manage the intricate components that make it work seamlessly. And that wizard can only be me.

The realization of my clients, that they had stumbled upon an extraordinary approach that had previously eluded them, further cemented their trust and belief in my capabilities. The results they witnessed firsthand served as a testament to the power of my methods, reinforcing the notion that they had made the right choice in partnering with me.

So, be prepared to experience the incredible. With me by your side, you can expect a pricing strategy that defies conventional norms and surpasses all expectations. The workload will be minimal, and the outcomes will be nothing short of extraordinary. I am the wizard you've been waiting for, ready to unleash my magical powers to drive your success to new heights.

Let me transport you to a moment that will forever be etched in the annals of print industry triumph. It was a time when a company found themselves facing an extraordinary challenge—a race against time with a seemingly insurmountable task ahead. A two-day deadline loomed ominously, demanding the pricing of a staggering 300 items. Doubt and despair crept in, casting a shadow of impossibility over the minds of the company's leaders.

But just when all hope seemed lost, a figure emerged from the shadows, donning celestial wings and an angelic crown. It was none other than me, the harbinger of possibility and master of the seemingly impossible. With a glint of determination in my eyes, I embarked on a heroic mission to turn the tides and lead the company to victory.

Sleep became a mere luxury as I dedicated myself to the task at hand. Time became an ephemeral concept, slipping through my fingers as I delved deep into the intricacies of each item. With unwavering focus, I meticulously analyzed the pricing structure, leaving no stone unturned. Every detail was scrutinized, every cost meticulously accounted for, and every opportunity for profit optimization carefully considered.

The magnitude of the challenge only fueled my resolve. I summoned an unyielding determination and unearthed an unparalleled wellspring of creativity. With each passing hour, I navigated the labyrinthine maze of pricing intricacies, crafting a strategy that would not only set the company apart but also defy the limits of what was thought to be possible.

The final hours dwindled, but my spirit burned brighter than ever. Exhaustion threatened to take hold, but I refused to succumb. With an unwavering commitment to excellence, I single-handedly forged a comprehensive and compelling proposal. The weight of the task was matched only by the sheer audacity of my efforts.

The moment of truth arrived—a crucial juncture where dreams either shatter or soar. The tender submission was made, carrying with it the hopes, aspirations, and untold hours of labor poured into every meticulously calculated price point. Nervous anticipation hung in the air as the company awaited the verdict that would determine their fate.

And then, like a crescendo building to a climax, the news arrived—triumphant and resounding. Against all odds, the company emerged victorious, securing the coveted contract they had dared to dream of. It was a testament to their unwavering spirit and the unwavering dedication I had poured into each and every calculation.

The exhilaration that filled the room was electric—a collective surge of joy, relief, and awe at the sheer magnitude of their achievement. The doubters were silenced, and the naysayers left in stunned silence. The name of the company reverberated through the industry, whispered in hushed tones as a symbol of unwavering determination and the power of collaboration.

But beyond the immediate triumph, the impact reverberated far and wide. The industry took notice, and whispers of my legendary prowess spread like wildfire. The tale of the impossible made possible by my skilled hands and unwavering resolve became the stuff of legend—a beacon of hope for companies facing their own Herculean challenges.

So, when you choose to work with me, be prepared to witness the unfolding of miracles. Together, we will shatter the boundaries of what is deemed possible, leaving a trail of triumphant victories in our wake. With wings of determination and a crown of expertise, we will navigate the treacherous seas of pricing challenges, secure contracts that were once deemed unattainable, and forever change the trajectory of your business.

Conquering the Print Tender Landscape

In the cutthroat world of print tendering, relying solely on tender platforms is a perilous mistake. The once-promising avenue has devolved into a treacherous labyrinth of missed opportunities and wasted efforts. The truth is, tender platforms have become overcrowded with hordes of competitors vying for the same tenders, drowning your chances of standing out. The days of uncovering hidden gems and exclusive opportunities through these platforms are long gone. To succeed in this ruthless landscape, a bold and unconventional approach is needed—one that leverages strategic marketing, innovative branding, and targeted outreach. Together, we will break free from the shackles of mediocrity and navigate the uncharted waters of print tendering, reclaiming the throne as the unrivaled champion of the industry.

So, prepare to be enlightened and transported into the extraordinary realm of print bidding mastery. Within this captivating world, there exists a formidable force—a bidding virtuoso who has shattered the boundaries of convention and unlocked the secrets to unrivaled success. As you embark on this exhilarating journey, behold the remarkable insights and transformative strategies that will forever change the trajectory of your bidding endeavors.

In a landscape teeming with print professionals who falter in their pursuit of lucrative tenders, our bidding luminary stands as a beacon of guidance and innovation. Casting aside the misguided notion that print contracts can be effortlessly attained through superficial measures, he has delved deep into the intricate tapestry of the procurement and tender industry, deciphering its enigmatic complexities with unparalleled acumen.

Gone are the days of futilely subscribing to print magazines or tender platforms, hoping for a serendipitous alignment with the ideal opportunity. Such passive approaches merely erect a barrier between you and the boundless profits that await. Our bidding sage knows this all too well, for he has witnessed firsthand the perils of wasted time and fruitless endeavors. He beckons you to cast aside these futile strategies and embark on a path that leads to resounding victories and unparalleled prosperity.

The world of print tender acquisition is one fraught with chaos and misalignment. Tenders are haphazardly published under incorrect categories, while paid tender platforms utilize erroneous feeds that obscure vital data and misdirect potential opportunities. The bidding arena becomes a labyrinthine maze, and the average print professional finds themselves adrift in an overwhelming sea of confusion. But fear not, for our bidding prodigy has the key to navigate these treacherous waters—a key forged through a decade of relentless determination, astute business acumen, and an unwavering commitment to uncovering hidden treasures.

At the core of his profound strategy lies an intricate web of meticulously planned maneuvers, an awe-inspiring blueprint that guarantees unrivaled success in sourcing tenders. Central to this remarkable framework is an all-encompassing dedication to a well-structured and highly detailed schedule, meticulously honed to perfection. No stone is left unturned as he meticulously scours the print tender landscape, leaving no opportunity unexplored. His profound strategy leverages the power of synergy, uniting market and sales teams in a harmonious symphony of bidding excellence.

Embracing the potential of integrated marketing communications, he orchestrates awe-inspiring campaigns that captivate the hearts and minds of procurers across the public and private sectors. With a dedicated micro-website serving as the epicenter of his bidding prowess, his brand emanates an irresistible allure, commanding attention and setting the stage for triumph. The culmination of these efforts breeds an irresistible allure that attracts all meaningful print tenders, even those hidden away deep within the recesses of the market.

But our bidding virtuoso's power does not end there. He possesses a unique talent for crafting case studies that transcend mere documentation, transforming them into compelling narratives that resonate with procurers on a profound level. By meticulously analyzing each project's nuances, he uncovers the intricate interplay of client needs, solution features, and team contributions. He masterfully weaves these elements into a tapestry of unparalleled persuasion, leaving competitors in awe and procurers captivated by the sheer brilliance of his approach.

His unwavering commitment to your success transcends the boundaries of conventional friendship. He becomes your confidant, your ally from a previous life, your guiding light in the dark abyss of the tender landscape. With a heart ablaze with unyielding devotion, he tirelessly works to secure your prosperity, sparing no expense or effort to ensure your triumph. He is not merely a bidder but a guardian of your business's destiny, an unwavering force that propels you towards unparalleled heights of success and happiness.

In the embrace of his extraordinary bidding expertise, your profits will soar, your dreams will be realized, and your legacy will be forever etched into the annals of print industry greatness. Prepare to embark on a journey that transcends the ordinary, as you are elevated to a realm where victory is the norm, and prosperity is your birthright.

In summary, dear reader, with our bidding virtuoso by your side, you will experience a revolution in your print business. His unmatched expertise in sourcing tenders and crafting winning bids will propel you to new heights of success. Together, you will navigate the complex tender landscape with ease, leaving your competitors in awe. So, join forces with this bidding mastermind and unlock the secrets to securing lucrative print contracts.

Prepare to embark on a remarkable journey where your dreams become a reality, guided by the unwavering dedication and unmatched talent of our bidding genius.

Behold the Unstoppable Force!

If you are in the print industry, my secrets will be invaluable to you. If you work in sales or marketing, you'll find yourself immersed in the powerful knowledge I possess. The incredible results I have achieved speak for themselves—winning print contracts worth £20 million or £50 million is no small feat, and I have done it single-handedly. What many fail to realize is that the workload involved in securing larger contracts is often similar to that of winning smaller ones. It still requires meticulous planning, organization, preparation, analysis, pitching, and outshining your competitors.

Now, you may be wondering, why do you need my secrets? Why do you need me? The answer is simple—by working with me, you eliminate the burdensome workload entirely. Instead of being bothered with all the intricacies and complexities of winning contracts, you can sit back and relax while I handle it all for you. Just imagine, leaning back and eagerly awaiting the influx of cash raining down upon your factory. I will be right there, ready to help you catch each and every opportunity with a bag. Together, we will navigate the competitive landscape, leaving your competitors in awe and securing a steady stream of lucrative contracts that will fuel the success of your print business.

Let me transport you into a world where the print industry undergoes a remarkable transformation, fueled by the relentless pursuit of excellence and the unleashing of my revolutionary approach.

Imagine a director of a print company, once burdened by the overwhelming task of winning print tenders, who eventually threw in the towel, weary from the countless hours spent on painstaking proposal preparations. In the beginning, it would take three grueling weeks to craft a single tender proposal, and even with experience, an entire week would be devoted to each endeavor. But alas, despite the valiant efforts, the tenders were elusive, slipping through their fingers like grains of sand. To add insult to injury, the print industry was plagued by the infuriating reality of low prices and narrow profit margins, casting a shadow of frustration upon the director's aspirations.

Yet, my friend, fear not, for the winds of change have swept through the print tender landscape, and with my arsenal of secrets, strategies, and industry expertise, we will conquer the pricing dilemma that has vexed the industry for far too long. As a print specialist, I possess a deep understanding of the intricacies and nuances of the print world. I am armed with the knowledge to create content that will leave our competitors quaking in their boots. Gone are the days of relying on others to create profits for you. With my guidance, you will seize the reins of your own destiny, watching in awe as your print business ascends to unprecedented heights.

Now, hold onto your seat as we delve into the exhilarating realm of collaboration. While I work harmoniously with sales and marketing teams, it is not to burden them with mundane queries or insurmountable tasks. No, my purpose is far grander. I bestow upon them the power of my extraordinary content, igniting a spark within their souls. Together, we unleash a tsunami of creativity, propelling us toward an abundance of new clients, captivating their attention with the sheer brilliance of our combined efforts. I encourage their active participation, for their triumphs become our triumphs, and together, we etch our names in the annals of greatness.

Let me unveil to you the awe-inspiring secret weapon at the heart of my triumphs—the art of crafting captivating case studies. These are not your ordinary run-of-the-mill accounts of projects completed. No, my friend, these case studies are masterpieces, meticulously designed to leave procurers breathless, their jaws agape with wonder. I dig deep into the essence of each client, unraveling their problems, needs, and desires with surgical precision. I forge an unbreakable connection, linking their journey to a tapestry of solutions, each thread woven intricately into the fabric of their success. I delve into the very soul of the project, examining every minute detail, scrutinizing the involvement of each team member. Their qualifications, their expertise, their unwavering dedication—all serve as the brushstrokes that paint a vivid portrait of excellence.

But wait, my friend, the spectacle does not end there. These case studies transcend the boundaries of ordinary storytelling. I expertly navigate the delicate realm of indirect comparisons, effortlessly pitting ourselves against competitors without uttering their names. The outcomes we achieve, the impact we create—it all unfolds in a breathtaking symphony of triumph. And as the crescendo builds, I unleash the final flourish—a resounding testimonial, an endorsement of our brilliance, uttered with unwavering conviction. The case study, presented in a visually stunning design, stands as a testament to our mastery, its very essence infused with the comprehensive features of the machinery we wielded to bring it to life.

Now, my friend, brace yourself for the ultimate revelation. These case studies, meticulously tailored to each tender proposal, radiate an irresistible allure. They draw procurers into our orbit, captivating them with their relevance, their depth, and their unparalleled attention to detail. No competitor can match our meticulously crafted narratives, our seamless blend of technical prowess and compelling storytelling. With every tender proposal we submit, we assert our dominance, commanding attention, and leaving procurers with no choice but to yield to our undeniable superiority.

So, my friend, if you seek to forge a path of unparalleled success in the print industry, if you yearn to conquer tenders with unrivaled brilliance, then join me on this exhilarating journey. Together, we will defy the norms, redefine the rules, and etch our names in the hallowed halls of victory.

The time for mediocrity is over—let us seize the future and revel in the sweet taste of triumph: asad@bidchampions.com.

Revolutionizing the Bid Process for Unmatched Success

Get ready to witness the transformative power of a bid champion who goes above and beyond traditional bid writing! While traditional bid writers simply rely on existing client content, I am here to revolutionize the bid process. As your bid champion, I take charge of the entire end-to-end bid journey, unlocking a world of possibilities for your business. Forget about the limitations of conventional bid writing— I bring a wealth of expertise and a wide range of services to ensure your bids stand out from the crowd.

Creating new and compelling content from scratch? It's my specialty. I craft impactful policies, captivating case studies, and persuasive presentations that captivate procurers and leave a lasting impression. But that's not all—I go the extra mile to forge new trade relationships, strengthening your pitch with unbeatable connections. My keen eye for detail allows me to align every aspect of your bid with the specific requirements of each invitation to tender, seamlessly addressing the wants and needs of the buyer.

But I don't stop there. I work hand in hand with your estimating department, developing innovative pricing strategies that give you a competitive edge. I keep a finger on the pulse of the market, continuously analyzing trends to optimize your bid pitches and solutions. When it comes to negotiations, I fearlessly advocate for your interests, skillfully navigating discussions with buyers, contracting authorities, and third parties.

Picture this—I personally present your bid, showcasing your unique value proposition with confidence and charm. I believe in building strong relationships, which is why I take the time to meet buyers face-to-face, establishing a genuine connection that sets you apart from the competition. And if challenges arise, worry not—I handle appeals and mediations with finesse, resolving conflicts and ensuring a fair outcome.

As your bid champion, I act as the bridge between stakeholders, coordinating efforts and ensuring everyone is aligned toward a common goal. When the need arises, I expertly bring together strong consortiums, leveraging the power of collaboration for maximum impact. Your bid presentation will never be the same—I continuously refine and improve it, injecting creativity and flair that captivates reviewers and leaves a lasting impression.

But I don't just stop at bidding—I bring a holistic approach to your business. With my expertise in procurement, I source top-notch suppliers who deliver exceptional quality and performance. I maintain and continuously enhance your bidding archives, making sure every piece of information is readily accessible and up-to-date. Together, we'll create and implement a winning bid strategy that propels your business forward, leaving competitors in the dust.

But my role doesn't end with bid submission. I seamlessly integrate new content into your existing marketing and sales processes, ensuring a cohesive and impactful approach across all touchpoints. I'm a data-driven professional, collecting and analyzing valuable insights to improve your overall business processes. From sourcing private and exclusive tenders to managing a non-stop bidding cycle, I am relentless in my pursuit of securing as many contracts as possible, increasing your yearly contract awards and fueling your growth.

So, are you ready to unleash the full potential of your bids?

Partner with me, your dedicated bid champion, and watch your success soar to new heights. Together, we'll conquer the bidding world, leaving a trail of victories in our wake.

Let's turn dreams into reality, one bid at a time: asad@bidchampions.com.

Unearthing Success in Single-Supplier and Framework Contracts

Prepare to be astounded by the depth and breadth of your bidder's expertise in differentiating between single-supplier and framework contracts. With a profound understanding of the unique strategies and approaches required for each, he has successfully navigated the complexities of tenders across a wide range of values.

When it comes to framework contracts, the average value of his successful wins has ranged between an impressive £1 million and a staggering £400 million. In fact, he has even secured a monumental framework tender worth an astonishing £1 billion, demonstrating his ability to handle large-scale and high-value contracts with confidence and finesse.

For single-supplier contracts, his track record is equally impressive. The average value of these contracts falls within the range of £1.5 million to £40 million, showcasing his proficiency in securing substantial projects that drive substantial growth for his clients. However, it is worth noting that he continues to secure a significant number of smaller contracts, including those valued between £200,000 and £500,000 (single supplier) and £500,000 to £1 million (frameworks), on a regular basis. Additionally, his unwavering commitment to success extends to micro-contracts, with wins ranging from £5,000 to £100,000 each year.

Throughout his tenure, he has successfully managed over 1000 tender projects using the esteemed PRINCE2 methodology, ensuring efficient and effective project execution. His ability to navigate the complexities of the bid management landscape has solidified his reputation as a seasoned professional capable of handling any challenge.

One of his greatest strengths lies in his uncanny ability to identify and source over 5000 suitable tenders across a wide array of platforms, gaining invaluable experience in multiple industries, including medical, recruitment, and print. This diverse knowledge base enables him to craft tailored and compelling bids that resonate with procurers across various sectors.

Recognized as an award-winning and creative profit magnet, he possesses a unique talent for crafting concise and impactful proposals. His succinct bidding style, combined with his unwavering dedication to securing victories, has made him a highly sought-after professional in the field. His expertise extends beyond bid management, as he regularly collaborates with C-level staff and effectively manages teams, ensuring seamless communication and coordination.

With a solid understanding of both private and public sector projects, he has honed his skills in preparing detailed and technical bids that leave a lasting impression. His prowess in developing pricing strategies and accurate estimations ensures optimal value for his clients, allowing them to achieve their goals while maximizing profitability.

His remarkable achievements include winning contracts valued at an astounding £1 billion in 2022, underscoring his ability to handle high-stakes projects with confidence and finesse. Moreover, he excels in building consortiums, strengthening company profiles, and forging strategic relationships that create a lasting impact, positioning his clients for long-term success.

Renowned for his ability to build and maintain robust pipelines, he consistently outperforms expectations, winning competitive Invitation to Tender (ITT) processes against all odds. His proven track record includes a wide range of bid types, such as RFPs, RFTs, and RFQs, solidifying his reputation as a formidable force in the bidding arena.

In addition to his exceptional bidding skills, he demonstrates a keen aptitude for resolving unforeseen challenges and meeting tight deadlines with ease. His ability to turn disadvantages into strengths showcases his resourcefulness and innovative thinking, ensuring you always remain ahead of the curve.

Throughout the bid process, he maintains open lines of communication, fostering strong relationships with you at every stage. His commitment to providing exceptional client experiences is evident in his development of over 300 win strategies, meticulously tailored to maximize success and deliver unmatched results.

Shortlisted for every tender and boasting a 100% success rate in the qualification stages over the past five years, he stands as a testament to his unmatched expertise and skill. With an impressive ITT win rate of 95% for the last 12 months, he is a proven leader in securing successful bids across a variety of bid types.

With his unwavering commitment to excellence, his adept coordination of proposal teams, and his organization of periodic strategy meetings, he ensures optimal use of time and resources, driving success at every stage of the bidding process.

Prepare to witness the extraordinary capabilities of this exceptional bid manager. With his expertise, passion, and unwavering dedication, your bid and proposal endeavors are destined for unparalleled success.

Reach out now: asad@bidchampions.com.

Your Catalyst: Amplifying Profits

Are you hesitant because you already have a bid process or a dedicated bidder in place? Let me make one thing clear: I don't care! I am here to provide unparalleled value and do whatever it takes to drive success for your business. With no risk or financial burden on your shoulders, I guarantee that I will propel your profits to new heights.

Imagine a scenario where your current bid process or bidder is already delivering results, but deep down, you have a burning desire for more. You know that there is untapped potential waiting to be unlocked, and that's where I come in. I am the ultimate catalyst, ready to unleash a wave of transformation that will revolutionize your bid process and elevate your profits to unprecedented levels.

If you already have a capable individual handling tenders, I will not replace them; instead, I will collaborate with them to amplify their efforts and triple the results. Together, we will create a synergy that goes beyond what either of us could achieve alone. By combining our expertise, experience, and strategic thinking, we will optimize your bidding strategies, uncover hidden opportunities, and outperform your competitors. With my guidance, your existing bidder will become an unstoppable force, armed with the tools and knowledge to secure even more lucrative contracts.

Now, let's consider the scenario where you have a full bidding department. It may be a well-oiled machine, but even the best teams can benefit from fresh perspectives and innovative approaches. As a seasoned bid professional, I will join your team as a valuable member, bringing a wealth of experience and a proven track record of success. I will seamlessly integrate into your existing structure, collaborating closely with your team members to identify areas for improvement, implement cutting-edge strategies, and enhance the overall performance of your bidding department. Through regular training sessions, I will impart valuable insights and best practices that will empower your team to become the best bidding team in the world.

Throughout my career, I have honed my skills in team formation, motivation, and conversion. I have witnessed firsthand the remarkable transformation that can occur when individuals come together, united by a shared goal and driven by a collective passion for success. I understand the dynamics of team dynamics and know how to foster a culture of excellence, collaboration, and continuous improvement. Whether your team needs a boost in morale, enhanced collaboration, or an injection of fresh ideas, I will be there to guide and support them every step of the way.

Now, you might be wondering, why should you consider me when you already have someone in place? The answer is simple: I am the catalyst that will take your bid process to extraordinary new heights. I am the embodiment of grandeur and power, capable of unleashing immense shockwaves of success that will reverberate throughout your organization. I am not just here to make incremental improvements; I am here to create a seismic shift in your bidding capabilities.

When it comes to profits, I am not talking about small gains or marginal improvements. I am talking about a significant increase in your bottom line that will have a transformative impact on your business. I will work tirelessly to ensure that every bid you submit is strategically crafted, meticulously tailored, and designed to maximize your chances of success. I will help you develop pricing strategies that optimize value, accurately estimate costs, and position you as the preferred choice for procurers. With my guidance, you will not only win more contracts but also secure high-value projects that drive substantial growth and catapult your business to new heights of success.

So, if you think you don't need me because you already have someone in place, think again. I am not just another bidder or bid consultant. I am the ultimate catalyst, the driving force that will propel your bid process to new horizons. Together, we will revolutionize the way you approach bids, outperform your competitors, and achieve unparalleled success.

Embrace the ultimate catalyst and embark on a journey of extraordinary growth and triumph: asad@bidchampions.com.

57

Your Personal Bid Ninja

Imagine a time when you found yourself amidst a team plagued by mistreatment and an unhealthy atmosphere. The weight of low expectations pressed down on your shoulders, and when challenges arose, blame and finger-pointing became the norm. It was a bleak and demoralizing experience, to say the least.

But then, someone extraordinary entered the scene - a catalyst for change, a beacon of hope. That someone was you. You stepped forward, ready to confront the root causes of the problem head-on. You knew that understanding the issues was the key to unlocking a better future, so you gathered the team for a pivotal meeting.

With unwavering determination, you fearlessly addressed the past and current issues, creating a safe space for every team member to share their thoughts and ideas. Your transparency and authenticity resonated with them as you shared your own personal struggles and triumphs. Slowly but surely, a shift occurred, and more and more team members found the courage to voice their opinions.

Together, you embarked on a transformative journey. Each issue was meticulously listed, and solutions were forged with the collective agreement of the team. This comprehensive overview brought a newfound sense of optimism, promising a bidding process that would be not only successful but enjoyable. Roles and responsibilities were assigned, and collaboration flourished as team members embraced the opportunity to support and learn from one another.

The remarkable change that ensued was nothing short of extraordinary. Your team members became more responsive, enthusiastic, and dedicated. You celebrated victories together, acknowledging and appreciating each individual's contribution to the process. The bidding arena was no longer a burden, but a playground for innovation and achievement.

Now, take a moment to imagine if this incredible transformation happened to you. If you were the catalyst for change, the one who inspired a team to rise above adversity and reach new heights. Wouldn't that be amazing?

Well, here's the thrilling revelation: That experience I just described—it happened to me. It happened because I had the audacity to challenge the status quo and the passion to ignite a revolution. I embraced my role as a leader and a visionary, and I want to share that same exhilarating journey with you.

No matter the size of the tender, I possess the unique ability to conquer it with finesse and unwavering determination. Whether you set your sights on a small-scale £5k or a substantial £50k opportunity, rest assured that I will emerge victorious. And if you dare to venture into the realm of larger contracts, be it a formidable £100k or a daunting £300k endeavor, I will secure success for you. Even the most audacious goals, such as tackling a monumental £500k or a breathtaking £2m bid, are within my realm of expertise. I possess the skills, experience, and strategic prowess to make your aspirations a tangible reality.

What sets me apart as the Flexible Bid Ninja is my hyperflexibility and innate ability to adapt to any bidding landscape. I possess an uncanny talent for pinpointing the exact workload and value you desire, honing in on the precise requirements with laser-like focus. My ninja-like abilities allow me to navigate the intricacies of the bidding process with unparalleled accuracy and finesse. Every aspect of your bid will be meticulously crafted, leaving no room for error. From crafting compelling proposals to strategically positioning your offering, I leave no stone unturned in my quest for victory.

Imagine a bidding process where your goals are not just met but exceeded, where your desires are transformed into tangible results with flawless precision. As the Flexible Bid Ninja, I possess the expertise and experience to tailor my approach to meet your unique needs, regardless of the tender's size or complexity. Whether you require a delicate touch for a smaller contract or a full-force assault for a major opportunity, I am equipped to deliver exceptional results.

Together, we will explore the exciting realm of bidding, unleashing our collective potential to achieve greatness. Allow me to showcase my ninja-like skills as we embark on this exhilarating journey. With the Flexible Bid Ninja by your side, you can navigate the bidding landscape with unwavering confidence, knowing that success is within reach.

Are you ready to harness the full power of the Flexible Bid Ninja and experience the thrill of bidding success? Reach out now to unlock the untapped potential of your bidding endeavors.

Let's leave our mark on the bidding world, rewriting the rules of engagement and seizing opportunities that others deem impossible.

The Flexible Bid Ninja eagerly awaits your call, ready to make bidding greatness a reality: asad@bidchampions.com.

Exploit This Resource

Prepare to embark on an extraordinary journey of bidding triumphs and unrivaled success. As a visionary and dynamic bid manager, I am here to ignite the fire within you, motivating you to push the boundaries of what's possible and achieve the impossible. Together, we will soar to new heights, leaving a trail of awe-inspiring achievements in our wake.

You possess untapped potential, and I am here to unlock it, to empower you to exploit every opportunity for greatness. Let's break free from the constraints of the ordinary and venture into the realm of extraordinary possibilities. I am not merely a bid manager; I am your ally, your catalyst, and your guiding light.

Imagine the thrill of surpassing your competitors, of securing contracts that were once deemed unattainable. Picture the joy of witnessing your business grow and flourish, as we navigate the intricate bidding landscape with finesse and determination. This journey is not just about winning contracts; it's about having fun, enjoying the process, and reveling in the exhilaration of achieving your dreams.

No challenge is too daunting, no deadline too tight. I thrive in the face of adversity, turning obstacles into stepping stones towards victory. Together, we will transform disadvantages into strengths, unveiling innovative strategies that set us apart from the competition. I am your partner in exploration, pushing the boundaries of what's possible, and daring to dream bigger than ever before.

Let's inject passion and excitement into every bid we undertake. Harnessing my expertise and unwavering dedication, we will create bids that captivate, inspire, and leave a lasting impression. We will infuse each proposal with a sense of adventure and ingenuity, ensuring that evaluators are captivated by our unique approach.

This journey is not just about financial gains; it's about unleashing your full potential and reveling in the joy of success. I am here to guide you, to mentor you, and to help you navigate the bidding landscape with confidence and finesse. Together, we will celebrate every victory, savoring the sweet taste of triumph and the satisfaction of a job well done.

Experience That Sets the Bar: With an extensive track record of managing over 2000 tender projects, I am the epitome of bid management excellence. I have mastered the esteemed PRINCE2 methodology, ensuring flawless project execution that propels us towards victory.

The Tender Whisperer: In my relentless pursuit of perfection, I have sourced and uncovered more than 2400 suitable tenders across a multitude of industries. My intimate knowledge of over 600 different tender platforms gives us a strategic advantage like no other.

Igniting Bids with Creativity: As an award-winning bid manager, I am celebrated for my innovative flair and masterful bid writing skills. I wield a succinct bidding style that captivates evaluators and leaves them yearning for more. No opportunity goes unnoticed, and I seize every moment to make our bid shine.

Industry Mastery at Your Service: From the intricate world of medical bids to the dynamic realm of recruitment and the captivating landscape of print, I possess an unparalleled understanding of these industries. This expertise allows me to craft bids that speak directly to the hearts of procurers, skyrocketing our chances of success.

Unleashing the Power of Relationships: Brace yourself for a collaborative journey with top-tier decision-makers. With a seamless rapport with C-level staff, I work hand in hand to shape strategies and conquer bidding challenges. As an experienced line manager, I inspire teams to reach their full potential, ensuring that our bids rise above the rest.

Precision in Pricing and Estimation: Maximizing profitability is an art form, and I am a master in the craft. I develop pricing strategies that leave our competitors trembling and estimations that are nothing short of impeccable. Together, we'll unlock the sweet spot where value and profitability intersect.

Conquering Giants: Picture the thrill of securing a contract valued at an awe-inspiring £1 billion in 2022. It's just one of the many remarkable triumphs I've achieved throughout my career. I have built consortiums, fortified company profiles, and forged alliances that create ripples of impact in the business world.

Thriving Against the Odds: I am no stranger to defying expectations and prevailing in the face of adversity. Building and maintaining full pipelines is my specialty, attracting profitable opportunities even in the most challenging circumstances. I have a knack for winning Invitation to Tenders (ITTs) against all odds, including the formidable RFPs, RFTs, and RFQs.

Mastering the Art of Supply Management: As a skilled practitioner of various supply management methodologies, I optimize efficiency and streamline operations. From strategic sourcing to logistics coordination, I bring order and effectiveness to every aspect of the bidding process.

Outshining Sales Professionals: Brace yourself for a revelation. I have outperformed entire sales departments, single-handedly generating more profits than nine full-time sales professionals combined. Prepare for a bidding journey that will transform the way you perceive business development.

Deadline Slayer and Challenge Overcomer: When the clock is ticking and unexpected hurdles arise, I am the calm amidst the storm. Tight deadlines fuel my drive, and I thrive in resolving unforeseen issues with ease. I possess the extraordinary ability to turn disadvantages into strengths, transforming obstacles into stepping stones towards triumph.

Unbreakable Client Connections: Expect unwavering dedication to maintaining a strong bond with clients throughout the bid process. Your goals and aspirations become mine, and together, we craft over 300 win strategies tailored to maximize success. You will feel the power of a bid manager who is by your side every step of the way.

Triumphing in Appeal Processes: Bid appeals hold no fear for me. I have successfully managed over 56 tender appeal processes, emerging victorious with an impressive 70% positive outcome rate. With my expertise, we'll navigate any roadblock and emerge triumphant.

Unstoppable Qualification Stages: I have been shortlisted for every tender and achieved a remarkable 100% success rate in the SQ/PQQ qualification stages over the past five years. When it comes to proving our worth, there's no one better equipped for the task.

A Winning Streak That Defies Gravity: Picture an ITT win rate of 95% over the last 12 months, encompassing a myriad of bid types such as RFPs, RFTs, and RFQs. I possess an indisputable track record that will instill confidence in your bidding endeavors.

So, my friend, are you ready to embark on this thrilling adventure? Are you prepared to push the boundaries, challenge the status quo, and achieve what others deem impossible? Let's seize the moment, embrace the excitement, and transform your bidding endeavors into a truly remarkable experience.

Contact me now and let the journey begin asad@bidchampions.com.

Together, we will make history, create unforgettable memories, and achieve the extraordinary. Get ready to unleash your potential and embark on a bidding journey like no other. The time for greatness is now.

How Much Will It Cost You?

Picture a world where print contracts hold the key to unimaginable profits and growth. It's not just about a small transaction for a trivial product; it's about securing long-term partnerships that bring in substantial revenue—£100k per year, or even an astounding £500k spread across multiple years. The possibilities are boundless, like discovering a treasure trove of gold ingots scattered throughout the print industry.

But with such incredible opportunities come challenges. It's easy to become overwhelmed by the desire for success and the immense fortune that awaits. That's where I come in—I will be your unwavering guide, your trusted partner, and your protector against the inner doubts and pitfalls that may arise. My role is to stabilize your spirit, helping you attract and handle the contracts that align with your capabilities. Together, we will embark on a journey of growth, step by step, project by project, until you become adept at handling an increased workload and reaping the rewards it brings.

Rest assured, I have carefully prepared backup plans to safeguard your interests. If ever you find yourself burdened by the weight of too many responsibilities, I will swiftly step in to alleviate the strain, allowing you to maintain focus and continue to profit handsomely. As you grow stronger and more confident in your abilities, I will ensure that you receive an ever-increasing stream of opportunities, tailored to your expanding capacity. With each new contract secured, your business will flourish, and I will be there every step of the way, shouldering the burdens and enabling your growth.

Now, you may wonder about the cost of accessing this wealth of knowledge and support. But let me assure you—my services are not a burden to your finances. If you don't win any print contracts, why should you pay me anything? It is not my intention to waste your time or resources. On the contrary, my purpose is to save you time, enable you to make money, and share in the prosperity we create together. Thus, all the work I invest in advance comes at no cost to you. I am confident in my ability to secure long-term print contracts that will generate substantial returns for your business.

So, with the knowledge that you are not required to make any upfront investments, you can confidently say YES to employing me as your personal bidder. Rest assured, I will use my incredible insight and dedicate my time to finding and securing the first print contracts for you. It will be a balanced approach, as I am committed to investing my evenings and weekends to realize these profitable sources of income on your behalf. I kindly ask for your patience during this process, as I meticulously navigate the tender landscape to ensure the best outcomes for your business.

However, should you feel a desire to accelerate the benefits and experience swifter and greater success, with wealth that will amaze not only yourself but also your friends and family, there is an alternative path we can explore. I am open to becoming a full-time team member, with compensation tied to the contracts you secure. This arrangement solidifies our partnership, allowing us to build a fair and successful relationship where we both share in the rewards of our collective efforts.

Embracing this alternative path will not only confirm our determination to succeed but also ensure your victory beyond any doubt. Your competitors will tremble in fear as we rise above them, leaving them in awe of our accomplishments. The unmatched level of success and prosperity we achieve together will be a testament to our unwavering commitment and drive.

Together, we will seize opportunities, conquer challenges, and elevate your business to unprecedented heights. Get ready to bask in the glory of victory, as we leave your competitors astounded and establish your business as a force to be reckoned with.

Let me be clear—both approaches are equally pure and blessed. They serve as the foundation for the beginning of our joint success story. Together, we will conquer the world of print contracts, achieving new heights of prosperity for your incredible business. So, let us embark on this remarkable journey, united in our pursuit of greatness and ready to

seize the boundless opportunities that lie ahead. I am ready
asad@bidchampions.com.

Elevate Your Print Business

The question on your mind is undoubtedly, "How soon can we begin?" Allow me to assure you that the wait is over. With unyielding determination and a burning desire for your bidding success, I stand ready to embark on this exhilarating journey by your side. As your personal bidding expert, I am committed to propelling your business to new heights and securing lucrative contracts.

From the moment you reach out to me at asad@bidchampions.com, we will waste no time in setting our plans into motion. Our collaboration begins with a comprehensive analysis of your bidding goals, aspirations, and unique business needs. With a deep understanding of your vision, I will tailor a bespoke strategy that aligns with your objectives and sets the stage for triumph.

Drawing upon my vast expertise in the realm of bidding, I will guide you through the intricacies of the bidding process, providing invaluable insights and strategic recommendations along the way. Together, we will craft compelling proposals that captivate the hearts and minds of procurers, setting you apart from the competition.

But it doesn't end there. As we embark on this journey, I am committed to being more than just a bidding consultant. I will be your confidant, your advocate, and your unwavering support system. With open lines of communication and a collaborative approach, we will work hand in hand, ensuring that your bidding efforts are executed flawlessly and yield exceptional results.

The path to bidding success may be challenging, but with my guidance, you can navigate it with confidence and ease. Whether it's refining your bidding strategies, fine-tuning your proposals, or conducting market research to uncover hidden opportunities, I am here to provide the expertise and support you need.

So, don't wait a moment longer. Take the leap and reach out to me at asad@bidchampions.com. Together, we will embark on a transformative journey, where your bidding endeavors will reach new heights and your business will flourish. The time for action is now, and I eagerly await your message, ready to make a lasting impact on your bidding success. Let's seize this opportunity and pave the way for a future filled with triumph and prosperity.

69